THE BENEFITS OF COLLECTIVE INTELLIGENCE

Make the most of your team's skills

Written by Véronique Bronckart
Translated by Emma Lunt

Coaching **50MINUTES**.com

50MINUTES.com

PROPEL
YOUR BUSINESS FORWARD!

NETWORKING

Effective CV Writing

Resolving Office Conflict

Boost Your Concentration

Find Your Work-Life Balance

www.50minutes.com

HOW TO USE COLLECTIVE INTELLIGENCE TO YOUR ADVANTAGE 1

COLLECTIVE INTELLIGENCE: THE BASICS 3

Collective intelligence in the workplace

The four forms of collective intelligence

What can be gained from collective intelligence?

Five ways to boost collective intelligence and gain six great abilities

Collective intelligence in management and group dynamics

The different levels of application of collective intelligence management

TOP TIPS 14

FAQS 16

Why use collective intelligence?

What is the aim of collective intelligence management?

What are the principles of collective intelligence management?

What are the obstacles to collective intelligence management?

What are the different perspectives on collective intelligence?

Is there a connection between collective intelligence and talent management?

Is there a difference between lean management and collective intelligence?

Is there a difference between collective intelligence and participatory management?

OVER TO YOU   21

FURTHER READING   26

HOW TO USE COLLECTIVE INTELLIGENCE TO YOUR ADVANTAGE

- **Issue:** what is collective intelligence and how can I take advantage of it in the workplace?
- **Uses:** collective intelligence enables a team to increase their efficiency, by making good use of each of its members.
- **Professional context:** team management, organisational management.
- **FAQs:**
    - Why use collective intelligence?
    - What is the aim of collective intelligence management?
    - What are the principles of collective intelligence management?
    - What are the obstacles to collective intelligence management?
    - What are the different perspectives on collective intelligence?
    - Is there a connection between collective intelligence and talent management?
    - Is there a difference between lean management and collective intelligence?
    - Is there a difference between collective intelligence and participatory management?

Of all the team management styles, the most innovative is unarguably that of collective intelligence. Not yet widespread in the vocabulary of corporate leaders, this new management method is currently facing some reluctance. Indeed, collective intelligence involves significant behavioural changes which have an impact on the culture, beliefs, skills, communication methods, organisation and functioning of the company.

Yet it is not always easy to face up to change and the uncertainty it brings. In a business world that is used to Taylorism, this new way of managing by accepting the novelty and diversity that each team member can bring is difficult to adopt as it opens new doors to knowledge and operating processes that have thus far not been explored by the organisation. The unknown is always a source of fear, and Taylorism allows us to avoid this by ensuring maximum control over actions and events to come.

The principles of collective intelligence go against Taylorism. In fact, the idea is to welcome novelties and the unknown, by accepting the risk of loss of control, but by gaining flexibility, reactivity and innovation. By interconnecting the differences and intelligence of each person, this method enables organisations to face up to unexpected events through reflection and collective action. Difficulties are resolved together, in the pursuit of a common goal.

In 50 minutes, discover the issues of collective intelligence and the reasons for which this management style is becoming an incontestable tool for promoting team efficiency.

COLLECTIVE INTELLIGENCE: THE BASICS

COLLECTIVE INTELLIGENCE IN THE WORKPLACE

Collective intelligence in the workplace consists of a group of managerial practices and behaviours that are based on the interactions between the various skills of workers in an organisation. It is not about simply being aware of the existence of the diverse skills of team members but also about understanding them and learning to optimally exploit them. This is done particularly by implementing a creation strategy incorporating group dynamics and the diversity of which it is made up. It is not just about communicating or assembling a team to put in place a process involving collective intelligence, but comprehending the rise of new intellectual resources, managing them and highlighting the experience and knowledge of each person.

It is important to differentiate between collective communication and collective reflection. Collective communication simply enables an exchange of information without calling upon the intellectual cooperation of each individual in a team. Collective reflection, in turn, involves intellectual cooperation, enabling the creation of information as well as giving it meaning and interacting with this information. This distinction is crucial as we often thinking we are cooperating when we are only communicating. Cooperating enables us to create synergies and make a decision based on the interactions of collective intelligence.

To sum up, it can be said that collective intelligence is the result of an interaction between the knowledge, skills and specific features of each individual in a group.

THE FOUR FORMS OF COLLECTIVE INTELLIGENCE

We traditionally distinguish four forms of collective intelligence. Indeed, collective intelligence is implemented differently, depending on the organisation in which it is practiced. The effectiveness of the method will also depend on the organisation's structure. By analysing the comparative table below, it is clear that the implementation of collective intelligence within a large, very hierarchical structure with pyramid-style management will be markedly less effective than in a small team.

The four forms of collective intelligence

Global collective intelligence	This is a fair, democratic, transparent, standardised and organised system, enabling the resolution of complex problems. This form is often found on the internet, particularly on social media platforms.
Original collective intelligence	This is the most well-known collective intelligence and the most used in the workplace, particularly during team meetings. It can be compared to the system put in place in a sports team, and thus primarily concerns small groups. It is the most advantageous form, as it is flexible, transparent, adaptable and open to improvisation.
Mass collective intelligence	It is this that we generally find within economic policies. The players interact without having a clear, overall vision of the system in which they develop. It needs more transparency and internal communication in order to be more effective.
Pyramid-shaped collective intelligence	This is regularly present within large structures such as public administration, multinationals or the banking sector. The vast majority of information is kept at the top. This collective intelligence is the least adapted to current issues, as it is rigid, restrictive and opaque.

WHAT CAN BE GAINED FROM COLLECTIVE INTELLIGENCE?

- **The creation of a value** or ethical code: this first benefit of collective intelligence reflects the fact that it promotes the development of the organisation and people.

In fact, it enables the organisation to develop its actions and projects while offering the individuals within it the chance for personal development. The act of soliciting and involving personnel in the implementation of new projects and decision-making by valuing each individual's skills enables everybody to gain self-confidence, find motivation and increase their efficiency. It is about being able to draw on the intelligence of group or organisation members and also to rally all external parties to the group or organisation (such as suppliers, clients and partners).

- **Information and communication:** different communication technologies make the exchange and sharing of information easier. They have to contribute to the increase in interactions by giving information an operational value.
- **Cooperation:** this is the most well-known method of materialising collective intelligence.
- **Knowledge management:** this is the foundation of optimal collective intelligence development and exploitation. Good management at this level enables the sharing and transfer of knowledge within a company.
- **The decentralisation of power and knowledge:** the leader is no longer the only one to have all the skills and to make decisions. They are collective.
- **Independence:** the individuals forming the team become stakeholders to achieve a common objective giving meaning to the group to which they belong.
- **Interaction:** interaction among members of a team – or a company – and the environment in which they develop (management, technology, economic policy) is constant.

FIVE WAYS TO BOOST COLLECTIVE INTELLIGENCE AND GAIN SIX GREAT ABILITIES

In order to begin the concept of collective intelligence and make it operational, it is imperative to interlink these five processes:

- **The cognitive aspect,** which involves creating a common goal together, based on a decision that is made collectively after understanding the issue and reflecting together. The key words regarding cognition within collective intelligence are:
  - mutual understanding (every group member expresses themselves freely and is understood by other members);
  - shared representation (each individual has their own representation of things or events and everybody is allowed the express themselves according to their own representation);
  - the use of a common language;
  - joint creation.
- **The relational aspect,** which involves ensuring that communication is clear and fully understood by each individual. It is also important to guarantee free and honest expression of every person as well as the open sharing of knowledge, perceptions and ideas. The relational element also requires the involvement of each individual, the recognition of the differences and skills of each person as well as the ability to adapt to this diversity.
- **The social aspect.** Collective intelligence is based on

various social aspects: active listening – meaning hearing what the other person says and understanding it – on the sharing and exchange of information and knowledge and on the functional organisation of the group. It also based on collaboration between different individuals that constitute a group, on self-confidence and confidence in others and on the independence of each person, among other things.

- **The managerial aspect,** as the effectiveness of collective intelligence depends on the size and composition of the group, how well its members complement each other, the tasks to accomplish and the components of the manager and the group.
- **The situation**, which leads to some external constraints and an organisational context which should be taken into consideration when implementing a collective intelligence management process.

For an organisation or team, the interaction of these five aspects enables six great abilities to emerge:

- understanding and reflecting collectively
- resolving problems collectively
- participating in decision-making
- creating a common vision
- promoting teambuilding
- motivating a team and getting its members involved.

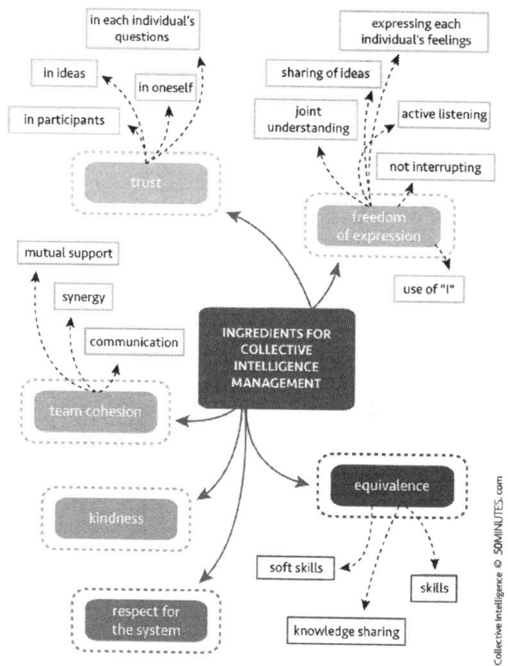

COLLECTIVE INTELLIGENCE
IN MANAGEMENT AND GROUP DYNAMICS

Being aware of the knowledge and skills of each individual in a team and learning to use these to your advantage enables you to increase the efficiency of the team. Collective intelligence is an undeniable management tool for promoting the exchange, sharing and exploitation of skills in the aim of achieving a common goal. Using collective intelligence is a progressive and participative team management style. Indeed, the role of a manager is not only being a leader that gives orders to their subordinates, but rather they become crucial for reinforcing the cohesion of their team by uniting them around reflections and shared actions. The leader thus becomes the "resources" person that shares their knowledge while welcoming the diversity of experience and skills of their team members.

Collective intelligence is a vital process in team dynamics. In fact, it leads to co-reflection, co-evolution and co-action, namely essential ingredients for promoting team dynamics by stimulating its members.

Collective intelligence and team dynamics

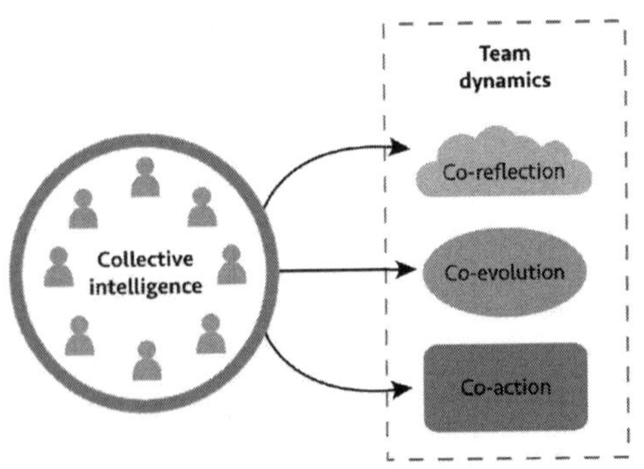

THE DIFFERENT LEVELS OF APPLICATION OF COLLECTIVE INTELLIGENCE MANAGEMENT

Collective intelligence management is not only a management tool for top managers. In fact, it is also strongly advised within the context of team management at all levels. Every person that is directing a team, whatever its size, can use collective intelligence. It is clear that when collective intelligence management is implemented by a supervisor, team leader or foreman it will often be more spontaneous than in the case of a process established by the manager, where it will generally take a more official form.

Steps to collective intelligence management implemented by a top manager	Steps to collective intelligence implemented by a team leader
<ul><li>Be aware of the different profiles that make up their organisation through human resources and meeting with team leaders.</li><li>Inform personnel, usually by a circular department notice, of their desire to implement collective intelligence management and call for a first informational meeting.</li><li>Gather all personnel and go around the table to do introductions. Allow each individual to express themselves freely about their private life, their feelings towards their role in the company, their skills, their experience, their passions, etc.</li><li>Welcome all this information and be aware of the diversity that is present within the organisation.</li><li>Implement a suggestion box (ex: invite personnel to write down what they suggest to improve the company's situation).</li><li>Gather the people that responded to the suggestion box and freely discuss, without judgement, each person's ideas then ask the participants to reflect on the ideas they have come up with.</li></ul>	<ul><li>Gather their team, inform them of their intention to implement collective intelligence management and clearly present the tasks that must be dealt with (ex: division of tasks).</li><li>Ask each person to speak freely about their feelings regarding their role in the team, the tasks they do, the way in which the team functions, their skills, their professional experiences, their passions, etc.</li><li>Welcome this information without judgement.</li><li>Encourage team members to bring forward their ideas either via a brainstorming during the meeting or by setting up a suggestion box.</li></ul>

Steps to collective intelligence management implemented by a top manager	Steps to collective intelligence implemented by a team leader
• During the subsequent meetings, which can be organised in sub-groups according to the topic or department concerned, give structure to the way the meeting plays out and attribute a role to each person (ex: leader, coordinator, note taker, etc.). • Have confidence and try to implement one of the suggested ideas. • Evaluate and solve any difficulties faced.	• Analyse and discuss the ideas together. • Implement the idea that has been brought up. • Evaluate and solve any difficulties faced.
A longer process which requires an atmosphere of trust within the company and an open-minded manager in order to enable personnel to express themselves freely and to detect the skills of each person.	A shorter and more spontaneous process, as the group is small and its members already know one another, which enables them to avoid certain obstacles that could be faced by a larger organisation.

TOP TIPS

- Start by defining a clear and reassuring vision for the members of your organisation by giving the people involved a chance to see both the internal and external potential benefits for the organisation.
- Ensure that trust and accountability are present within the organisation to enable the sharing and exchange of the understanding of these potential benefits. You can thus promote team cohesion and unite them around a common goal that is defined together.
- Share information and communicate the knowledge and experiences of each person.
- In order to make team cohesion and collective intelligence easier, offer opportunities for formal or informal encounters between different members of the team or organisation, particularly through meetings, training, seminars, team building or other activities.
- No longer think of yourself as the most competent in all areas, but invite your colleagues to establish themselves as competent individuals and to share their knowledge through communication and exchange, so as to produce a collective creation. Collective intelligence is also the synergy of each person. It is essential that you are open to others, that you accept and understand different points of view and that you incorporate the innovations brought by each person by facilitating everybody's input. In this way, use collective language, particularly by using "we".
- Embody particular values and become a 'human resource' by listening to your team, while offering your services

to others. Emphasise active listening and empathetic understanding among people.

- Allow the team to learn, evolve, reflect and act together, in synergy. Support them mutually, excuse them in case of errors and try to resolve problems collectively.
- Do not hesitate to enlist the help of a professional who will bring a necessary external view to avoid inconsistencies. This help can be in the form of a managerial committee involving meetings, progress reports and indications of the results, which enables team development through feedback. Coaching can also be an ideal form of support as it influences behaviour, attitude and procedures.

AT A GLANCE

Collective intelligence cannot be the result of a simple organisational change, of merely a personal change on the part of the manager or an attempt to implement a new management method from the top-down. It has to be the result of communication between all stakeholders.

FAQS

WHY USE COLLECTIVE INTELLIGENCE?

Collective intelligence is a useful tool for optimising the efficiency of a team. In fact, assembling and exploiting all the knowledge and skills of different team members amplifies the team's abilities. Not only does this allow them to take advantage of each person's strengths, but it also strongly increases individuals' motivation by involving them in decision-making and by recognising and valuing their skills. Furthermore, making use of different skills and experiences enables certain problems to be resolved internally without resorting to external involvement, and therefore avoiding additional costs and saving time.

Collective intelligence also enables better talent management and therefore better task division so as to optimise each person's efficiency, as well as that of the team as a whole.

WHAT IS THE AIM OF COLLECTIVE INTELLIGENCE MANAGEMENT?

The aim of this type of management is to make intelligent decisions based on the development of ideas and solutions by all the people that are affected by these decisions.

WHAT ARE THE PRINCIPLES OF COLLECTIVE INTELLIGENCE MANAGEMENT?

The principles of collective intelligence management are essentially as follows:

- Implement an idea of equivalence, meaning emphasising that the diversity of skills, experiences and soft skills is an asset for the whole organisation or team.
- Adopt active listening, which means listening attentively to what the other person says by allowing them to express their ideas without interrupting before they are finished.
- Invite participants to speak with intention, meaning to speak as their own person by using "I" and avoiding any generalisation caused by using "we".
- Do not judge but be kind, by realising that there is no such thing as a good or bad participant or a bad idea. On the contrary, even an idea that is theoretically mediocre can cause reactions and exchanges that lead to the development of a solution.
- Be confident in the group of participants and yourself, as well as in the ideas that you all come up with, as it is the people as a whole, their ideas and their questions that enrich the communal fund.
- Respect the system that is bringing everybody around to the principles cited above.

WHAT ARE THE OBSTACLES TO COLLECTIVE INTELLIGENCE MANAGEMENT?

The main obstacles to implementing collective intelligence are cultural. Before throwing yourself into a management process of collective intelligence, it is essential to ensure that this corresponds with the organisation's managerial culture. If this is not the case, you will need to raise awareness among the hierarchy and all the people concerned in order to mould the organisation's culture and prepare it for this type of management. The managerial style must be revised. It is suitable to change some operating processes such as the hierarchy's lack of involvement, refusing interdisciplinary communication, management centred around the individual and not on the group effect, etc. It is very difficult to implement effective collective management within an organisation whose management style is pyramid-shaped.

It will also be necessary to work on inherent obstacles within each individual, such as the fear of change, fear of criticism, fear of having to make more effort, competitive spirit, individualism and perfectionism.

WHAT ARE THE DIFFERENT PERSPECTIVES ON COLLECTIVE INTELLIGENCE?

In an organisation, collective intelligence enables the creation of a democratic company within which every decision is made by the majority. Collective intelligence contributes to the development of decisions but does not impact decision-making. It is not about the redistribution of power, but a change in management style which involves valuing all the diversity in the knowledge, skills and ideas of individuals in an organisation or team in order to unite them in a constructive and effective manner.

IS THERE A CONNECTION BETWEEN COLLECTIVE INTELLIGENCE AND TALENT MANAGEMENT?

Yes, collective intelligence uses skills by combining them and enabling them to show the best of each person. When an organisation bets on collective intelligence and the involvement of its people in the implementation of actions or decision-making, it has the chance to detect each individual's performance. Collective intelligence thus becomes a facilitator or talent director: it can offer a person the chance to participate in projects that are different from their everyday tasks.

IS THERE A DIFFERENCE BETWEEN LEAN MANAGEMENT AND COLLECTIVE INTELLIGENCE?

Yes. Lean management is an organisational approach which enables Taylorism to be pushed even further by ensuring control is kept. Lean management aims to improve the organisation's performance by developing all the employees (training, motivation), with the main objective being total client satisfaction and consequently, increased turnover. Lean management seeks to constantly improve the performance of individuals and processes while reducing costs as much as possible. This can be summarised as 'efficiency and profitability' with no possible error.

In terms of collective intelligence, it is a relational approach which counts on the synergy of skills and knowledge in order to create strategies together and develop collective performances. Collective intelligence accepts the loss of control and draws on lessons learned from potential mistakes in order to resolve them collectively.

IS THERE A DIFFERENCE BETWEEN COLLECTIVE INTELLIGENCE AND PARTICIPATORY MANAGEMENT?

There is a thin line between these two methods. Participatory management aims to carry out a personnel development process by involving them in the implementation of projects within the organisation and in decision-making. It requires the ability to delegate power and to trust its team with the resolution of different issues. In this way, participatory management inevitably reminds us of collective intelligence, but goes further than the latter in overall organisational reflection. Collective intelligence is therefore a means of reaching a participatory management process.

OVER TO YOU

Develop collective intelligence in your team in eight steps.

STEP ONE

Identify your team. Close your eyes and think of each person in the team. Who are they? What are they passionate about? What motivates them? What do they expect from you? What are their skills and experience? How can these skills be brought together? Where and in what way is it possible to combine them?

STEP TWO

Ensure that the team members understand the intentions of this joint action. Clearly explain your objective and ask for their opinion. Formalise the place, pace and context in which the group will come together to co-initiate the pilot project.

STEP THREE

Encourage a sudden collective awareness by organising a meeting without anything on the agenda. Bring together the people that have shown great interest in your collective intelligence management project. Go around the table and allow them to speak about what is happening within the organisation, their team, maybe their private life. Stay open-minded. Freely discuss the work and challenges of the organisation by discovering the new ideas, interests

and motivations of each person. Conclude the meeting by
coming up with a pilot program with a common vision.

STEP FOUR

Plan your upcoming meetings. If they last an hour, plan:

- time to present the issue to be dealt with during the
  meeting (around 5 minutes)
- a relatively long space of time for reaction and exchange
  (around 40 minutes)
- and end with a conclusion (10 minutes maximum).

STEP FIVE

At the start of each week, gather your team together.

- Give each participant a role in the meeting. Designate a
  leader who explains the case to the group (they should
  be chosen according to the subject), a facilitator who
  will incite the discussion, a timekeeper. You can also
  call on a coach for an external view and expertise of the
  organisation.
- Ask each member to share their ideas on the chosen issue
  (work, organisation, company projects). Welcome these
  ideas and chase them up during the week by asking each
  person to reflect on these ideas.

STEP SIX

At the end of the week, meet again and share your conclusions on the received ideas and welcome new ideas that

come from these conclusions. Repeat this until one or many ideas are unanimously agreed to.

STEP SEVEN

Implement the new ideas.

STEP EIGHT

Evaluate the actions put into place together and collectively reflect on the solutions to be implemented in case of failure.

Summary

1. Identify each member of your team and their skills.

2. Explain your objective to them.

3. Organise a meeting with nothing on agenda.

4. Plan your next meetings.

5. Plan an open meeting at the start of the week.

6. At the end of the week, come back to the ideas that were previously thought of.

7. Implement the ideas that are agreed to unanimously.

8. Collectively evaluate the actions put into place.

FURTHER READING

BIBLIOGRAPHY

- Devillard, O. (2005) *Dynamiques d'équipes*. Paris: Éditions d'Organisation.
- Greselle, O. Z. (2007) Vers l'intelligence collective des équipes de travail: une étude de cas. *Management & Avenir*. [Online]. 4(14), pp. 41-59. [Accessed 9 November 2016]. Available from: <http://www.cairn.info/revue-management-et-avenir-2007-4-page-41.htm>
- Zara, O. (2007) Le management de l'intelligence collective. Paris: M21 Éditions.

ADDITIONAL SOURCES

- Bouvard, P. and Suzanne, H. (2017) *Collective Intelligence Development in Business*. London: ISTE Ltd.
- Dilts, R. B. (2016) *Generative Collaboration: Releasing the Creative Power of Collective Intelligence (Success Factor Modeling)*. California: Dilts Strategy Group.
- Malone, T. W. and Bernstein, M. S. (2015) *Handbook of Collective Intelligence*. Cambridge (Massachusetts): Massachussetts Institute of Technology.